DREAM
The Ex
Jacqu

by Ann Sreyts • illustrated by Jack Crane

Chapters

Harcourt

Orlando   Boston   Dallas   Chicago   San Diego

Visit *The Learning Site!*

www.harcourtschool.com

Introduction

A man in a red woolen cap stared into the distance as he breathed in the fresh, salt air. His ship was headed toward the Red Sea. To this man, the ocean was a wild and beautiful frontier.

The man was Jacques Cousteau, one of the greatest explorers and inventors of the last century. He was sailing on his ship *Calypso* to learn more

Cousteau aboard the *Calypso*

about life in the ocean. Through his work, Jacques Cousteau showed the world its oceans as they had never been seen before. He died in 1997, but his contributions to what we know about the sea are very much alive today.

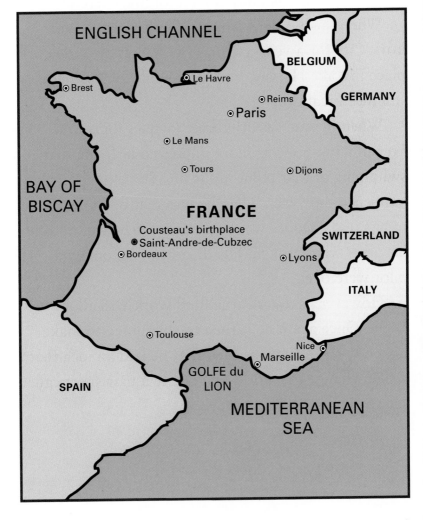

Growing Up

Jacques Yves Cousteau was born in France in 1910. He was born with a disease that made him weak. However, Jacques did not let that discourage him. He swam to keep his body strong and grew to love the water. His body thrived on the exercise.

When Jacques was ten, his family lived in New York City for a year. Jacques's very first dive took place in Lake Harvey, Vermont, while he was on a summer vacation.

When he was twenty-three, Jacques joined the French navy. He was more interested in flying than swimming at that point in his life. Something terrible happened, however, when he was ready to take his pilot's test. Jacques was in a car accident and both of his arms were broken. His dreams of becoming a pilot were over.

However, Jacques's true life's work was about to begin. Once again he turned to swimming to make his body strong. It was then that he had an idea that would change the world and create a new sport called scuba diving.

Cousteau's Most Famous Invention

Jacques began thinking of ways he could breathe under water. He built an air "breather" made of oxygen and soda cans. Unfortunately, this equipment proved almost deadly.

Jacques didn't give up, though. He was sure he could make a machine for breathing under the water. He worked on another version of an air breather with engineer Emile Gagnan. They constructed the very first aqualung in 1943. It is known today as *SCUBA* (self-contained underwater breathing apparatus). The apparatus was made of three tubes that held compressed air. It also had a valve to adjust the air flow. A gauge was added later that let divers know how deep in the ocean they were.

Cousteau and his famous aqualung

With the aqualung, Jacques could stay underwater for a long time. Divers could now move around more freely in deep water.

0'
1'
2'
3'
4'

With the invention of the aqualung, divers were able to adjust their buoyancy.

Cousteau's machine solved another problem for divers. The human body has a natural ability to float. Before this invention, divers weren't able to reach great depths without floating back up to the water's surface. With the aqualung, divers could adjust their buoyancy to make deeper dives.

Jacques's new and important breathing machine quickly received worldwide attention. France used the equipment to salvage dangerous mines left in the ocean after World War II. Special diving teams formed by Jacques and his friend Philippe Taillez did this dangerous task.

Cousteau saw various beautiful forms of marine life up close.

Films, Television, and Books

Jacques was very excited about his new invention and dived whenever he could. He was amazed by the diversity of the marine life he saw. In his many dives, he saw unusual plants and animals. He even watched large schools of fish dissipate when dolphins gathered.

Jacques built a waterproof case for his camera and recorded the beauty he saw. In his lifetime, he made over one hundred films of his adventures in the ocean. They won many awards, including an Oscar for *The Silent World*.

Jacques also created five television series. The most well-known was called *The Undersea World of Jacques Cousteau*. This show presented the different plants and animals Cousteau met in his journeys on the *Calypso*.

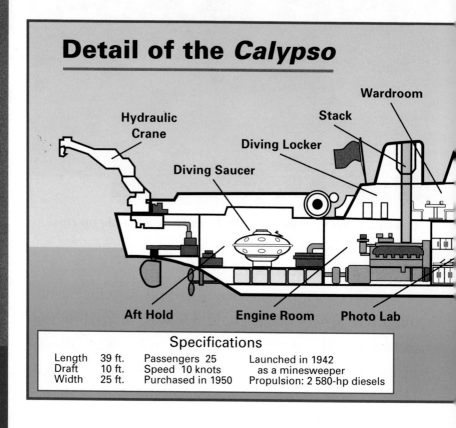

Detail of the *Calypso*

Hydraulic Crane

Wardroom

Stack

Diving Locker

Diving Saucer

Aft Hold

Engine Room

Photo Lab

Specifications

Length	39 ft.	Passengers 25	Launched in 1942
Draft	10 ft.	Speed 10 knots	as a minesweeper
Width	25 ft.	Purchased in 1950	Propulsion: 2 580-hp diesels

The first show in this series followed Jacques and his team as they learned about sharks. Other shows in the series examined whales and other marine life. In 1973 the series covered a concert of whales singing. The acoustic ability of these humpback whales was recorded in the West Indies.

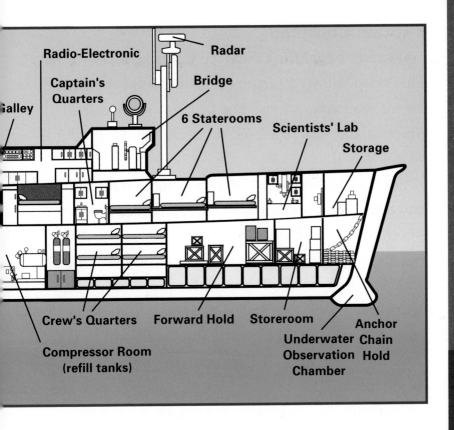

Radio-Electronic
Radar
Captain's Quarters
Bridge
Galley
6 Staterooms
Scientists' Lab
Storage
Crew's Quarters
Forward Hold
Storeroom
Anchor Chain Hold
Compressor Room (refill tanks)
Underwater Observation Chamber

Jacques Cousteau also wrote many books for both adults and children. In his books, he told about his many exciting adventures in places such as the Amazon River and the Red Sea. His books have been printed in more than twelve languages, so people all over the world can read his personal thoughts on his expeditions. They also can learn about Jacques's love of the ocean.

Captain Cousteau

Jacques bought his ship, the *Calypso*, in 1950. This vessel allowed Jacques to sail around the world for his sea explorations. The *Calypso* was made in America and was first used to salvage mines during World War II.

Jacques had dreamed of a ship that would help him learn more about the ocean. He added a room where he could observe the underwater scene. A lab and space for dive gear were also put on the ship.

On one trip to the Red Sea, Jacques and his crew discovered a ship that had sunk over two thousand years before. Ancient Greek statues were salvaged from the ocean floor. This was an important historical discovery.

Most of Jacques's films were made while sailing on the *Calypso*. In 1952, he shot the first color film 150 feet beneath the water's surface. His films were interesting to many people because they showed real-life adventures.

Jacques explored the world's oceans on the *Calypso* for many years. He even went to Antarctica, where he was caught in a snowstorm. It was there in 1972 that he found ice formed beneath the water. The film of this adventure was shown on television.

Jacques had many adventures on the *Calypso*. He sailed the *Calypso* to Easter Island, off the coast of Chile. He sailed it to Yugoslavia, where he was caught in a war. He sailed it to Madagascar. He even sailed the *Calypso* on the Mississippi River in the United States.

Jacques sailed the *Calypso* for almost four decades. The ship is now on permanent display at the Maritime Museum in France.

Cousteau and the *Calypso* sailed around the world for four decades.

Cousteau explaining the *Conshelf I* experiment

Living Under the Sea

While Jacques was still enjoying his adventures aboard the *Calypso*, he realized he wanted to learn even more about the ocean. He was determined to find a way for people to *live* underwater at great depths. Jacques began what were called the "Conshelf experiments." The experiments were given this name because they took place on the continental shelf. The continental shelf is a land ledge beneath the ocean. Every continent has one. In some places, it is 600 feet below the surface.

The *Conshelf I* experiment took place off the coast of France in 1962. Two men lived below the surface in a cylinder for one week. Jacques was the director of the experiment, so he was not one of the divers.

The second experiment was called *Conshelf II*. In June 1963, five men lived thirty-five feet below the surface of the Red Sea. They lived there for an entire month. The underwater shelter was called Starfish House. The men enjoyed air-conditioning and scenic views through special windows. They even ate delicious meals.

Conshelf III took place in 1965. Six men lived 330 feet down in the Mediterranean Sea. This was much deeper than the *Conshelf II* experiment. Jacques's son Philippe was one of the divers. They were called oceanauts

because they were exploring unknown territory. They stayed underwater for three weeks.

Honors and Awards

Jacques Cousteau's hard work did not go unnoticed. He received awards for his efforts throughout his life.

Many countries honored Jacques for his important discoveries and inventions. He won two medals for his work during World War II. In 1977, he won the Environmental Prize of the United Nations. Then, in 1985, he won the United States Presidential Medal of Freedom. President Ronald Reagan presented Jacques with the medal. France acknowledged him as its official oceanographer. That country also recognized Jacques as one of the greatest contributors to French culture. Universities in several countries also gave Jacques honorary degrees.

Many people remember Jacques best for his television series. *The Undersea World of Jacques Cousteau* won several Emmy awards. His work on television was so respected that he was inducted into the Television Academy of Fame in 1987.

14

Protecting the Environment

Throughout his diving career, Jacques admired the beauty of the plants and animals he observed under the sea. He wanted future generations to have the opportunity to see them as well. He knew that the water needed to be clean in order to support humans and wildlife. So he became involved in protecting the oceans.

In 1974, Jacques formed the Cousteau Society. The society raised money to fund explorations. This allowed Jacques to educate people about the condition of the oceans and get them to help solve the pollution problem.

Today many schools and other groups participate in cleaning oceans shores and local streams. School volunteers participate in the regular clean-ups. Students learn that they play a large part in improving the condition of the oceans.

Final Thoughts

Jacques Cousteau once said, "There is not a bad dive. Never. Always something new to learn and see."

Jacques wanted to make the ocean available to everyone—not just to scientists. He did just that and more. With his creation of the sport of scuba diving, people of all ages and backgrounds could dive and move like fish beneath the ocean's surface. His work to protect the water helped to continue this dream.

Jacques Cousteau was an inventor and an explorer. He was also a dreamer. His interests as a child led him to become an important person in history. Jacques Cousteau did more than invent a diving machine. He taught the world how to use it.